*Preparing a List of Works Cited* **S-3**

your instructor asks you to follow the style of the *MLA Handbook,* 2nd ed.

Unless your instructor specifies otherwise, list only those sources that you actually cite in the body of the paper, not sources that you examined but do not cite. Arrange the sources alphabetically by the author's last name. Two or more works by the same author should be alphabetized under the author's name by the first main word of the title (that is, excluding *a, an,* or *the*). Anonymous sources should be alphabetized in the list by the first main word of the title.

Place the list of works cited at the end of your research paper. Double-space all the entries, and indent the second and subsequent lines of each entry five spaces. See page S-34 for an illustration of the "Works Cited" form in an actual research paper.

## *Books*

**A BOOK WITH ONE AUTHOR**

Kael, Pauline. <u>Deeper into Movies</u>. Boston: Atlantic-Little, Brown, 1973.

**TWO OR MORE BOOKS WITH THE SAME AUTHOR**

Gardner, Howard. <u>The Arts and Human Development</u>. New York: Wiley, 1973.

---. <u>The Quest for Mind: Piaget, Lévi-Strauss, and the Structuralist Movement</u>. New York: Knopf, 1973.

**A BOOK WITH TWO OR THREE AUTHORS**

Wimsatt, William K., and Cleanth Brooks. <u>Literary Criticism: A Short History</u>. Chicago: U of Chicago P, 1978.

**A BOOK WITH MORE THAN THREE AUTHORS**

Lopez, Robert S., et al. <u>Civilizations: Western and World</u>. Boston: Little, Brown, 1975.

**A BOOK WITH CORPORATE AUTHORSHIP**

Editors of <u>The Progressive</u>. <u>The Crisis of Survival</u>. Glenview: Scott, Foresman, 1970.

**A LATER EDITION**

Bollinger, Dwight L. <u>Aspects of Language</u>. 2nd ed. New York: Harcourt, 1975.

**A REPUBLISHED BOOK**

James, Henry. <u>The Golden Bowl</u>. 1904. London: Penguin, 1966.

### A WORK IN MORE THAN ONE VOLUME

Lincoln, Abraham. The Collected Works of Abraham Lincoln. Ed. Roy P. Basler. 8 vols. New Brunswick: Rutgers UP, 1953.

Lincoln, Abraham. The Collected Works of Abraham Lincoln. Ed. Roy P. Basler. 8 vols. New Brunswick: Rutgers UP, 1953. Vol. 5.

### A TRANSLATION

Alighieri, Dante. The Inferno. Trans. John Ciardi. New York: New American Library, 1971.

### A WORK IN A SERIES

Bergman, Ingmar. The Seventh Seal. Modern Film Scripts Series. New York: Simon and Schuster, 1968.

### A BOOK WITH AN EDITOR

Spradley, James P., and David W. McCurdy, eds. Conformity and Conflict. 4th ed. Boston: Little, Brown, 1980.

### A BOOK WITH AN AUTHOR AND AN EDITOR

Melville, Herman. The Confidence Man: His Masquerade. Ed. Hershel Parker. New York: Norton, 1971.

### A SELECTION FROM AN ANTHOLOGY

Twain, Mark. "The War Prayer." The Complete Essays of Mark Twain. Ed. Charles Neider. Garden City: Doubleday, 1963. 679-82.

### A SCHOLARLY ARTICLE OR ESSAY FROM A REPRINTED COLLECTION

Evan, W. M. "Due Process of Law in Military and Industrial Organizations." Administrative Science Quarterly 7 (1962): 187-207. Rpt. in The Managerial Dilemma. Ed. Stephen K. Banks. New York: Interface, 1980. 234-50.

## *Periodicals: Journals, magazines, and newspapers*

### A SIGNED ARTICLE IN A JOURNAL WITH CONTINUOUS PAGINATION THROUGHOUT THE ANNUAL VOLUME (SEE P. 455)

Gubar, Susan, and Anne Hedin. "A Jury of Our Peers: Teaching and Learning in the Indiana Women's Prison." College English 43 (1981): 779-89.

**A SIGNED ARTICLE IN A JOURNAL THAT PAGES ISSUES SEPARATELY OR THAT NUMBERS ONLY ISSUES, NOT VOLUMES (SEE P. 455)**

Boyd, Sarah. "Nuclear Terror." Adaptation to Change 7 (1981): 20-23.

**A SIGNED ARTICLE IN A MONTHLY OR BIMONTHLY PERIODICAL**

Stein, Harry. "Living with Lies." Esquire Dec. 1981: 23.

**A SIGNED ARTICLE IN A WEEKLY OR BIWEEKLY PERIODICAL**

Katz, Donald R. "Drawing Fire: Cartoonist Bill Mauldin and His 35-Year Fight for Truth, Justice, and the American Way." Rolling Stone 4 Nov. 1976: 52+.

**A SIGNED ARTICLE IN A DAILY NEWSPAPER**

Bowman, David. "Wrath: My Cow O'Leary's Plan for a Greater Memphis." Center City 11 Nov. 1976: 1-2.

**AN UNSIGNED ARTICLE**

"500 March Against Death Penalty." Boston Sunday Globe 13 May 1979, sec. 1: 21.

"Notes on Personal Computers." Microcomputer 2 (1980): 242.

"The Right to Die." Time 11 Oct. 1976: 101.

## *Encyclopedias and almanacs*

**AN UNSIGNED ARTICLE IN AN ENCYCLOPEDIA**

"Mammoth." The New Columbia Encyclopedia. 1975 ed.

**A SIGNED ARTICLE IN AN ENCYCLOPEDIA**

Mark, Herman F. "Polymers." Encyclopaedia Britannica: Macropaedia. 1974.

## *Bulletins, pamphlets, and government documents*

Zasloff, J. J. "Origins of the Insurgency in South Vietnam, 1954-1960." RAND Corporation Collection RM-4703/2-ISA/ARPA. Santa Monica: RAND, 1968.

Resource Notebook. Washington: Project on Institutional Renewal Through the Improvement of Teaching, 1976.

National Endowment for the Humanities. "National Endowment for the
Humanities Education Program Guidelines, 1978-1979."
Washington: GPO, 1978.

United States. Dept. of Labor. Employment and Earnings 27.9
(1981): 18-20.

## *Unpublished dissertations and theses*

Wilson, Stuart M. "John Stuart Mill as a Literary Critic."
Diss. U of Michigan, 1970.

## *Films and television programs*

Allen, Woody, dir. Manhattan. With Allen, Diane Keaton, Michael
Murphy, Meryl Streep, and Anne Byrne. United Artists, 1979.

King of America. Writ. B. J. Merholz. Music Elizabeth Swados.
With Larry Atlas, Andreas Katsulas, Barry Miller, and Michael
Walden. PBS American Playhouse. WNET, New York. 19 Jan. 1982.

## *Plays and concerts*

Richard III. By William Shakespeare. Dir. David Wheeler. With
Al Pacino. Cort Theatre, New York. 28 June 1979.

Ozawa, Seiji, cond. Boston Symphony Orch. Concert. Symphony Hall,
Boston. 25 Apr. 1982.

## *Recordings*

Mitchell, Joni. For the Roses. Asylum, SD 5057, 1972.

Brahms, Johannes. Concerto no. 2 in B-flat, op. 83. Audiotape.
Perf. Artur Rubinstein. Cond. Eugene Ormandy. Philadelphia
Orch. RCA, RK-1243, 1972.

## *Interviews*

Smithson, Councilman John. Personal interview. 6 Sept. 1980.

## *Computer software*

MultiMate 3.2. Computer software. SoftWord Systems, 1984. IBM PC,
192KB, disk.

# S2
## Citing sources with parenthetical references

If your instructor asks you to use the documentation system of the *MLA Handbook*, 2nd ed., you will employ parenthetical references to sources instead of the endnotes or footnotes explained on pages 480–87 of the text. Note that you will have to prepare your list of works cited before you can insert the final parenthetical references in the draft of your paper. While you are drafting the paper, make a note of where each citation should appear and of what should be cited (author's name, page number, and other necessary information) so that the final references can be inserted easily and accurately just before you prepare the final draft for submission.

### What to include in a parenthetical reference

The in-text references to sources must include (a) just enough information for the reader to locate the appropriate source in your list of works cited, and (b) just enough information for the reader to locate the place in the source where the borrowed material appears. Usually, you can meet these requirements by providing the author's last name and the page in the source on which the material appears:

    One prominent film critic holds that "movies, by affecting us on
    sensual and primitive levels, are a supremely pleasurable--and
    dangerous--art form" (Kael xvii).

With the information provided in parentheses, the reader can find Kael's book in the list of works cited and find the quotation in the book itself. (The page in this case is one numbered with small Roman numerals.)

If the author's name is already given in the text, you need not repeat it in the parenthetical reference:

    One prominent film critic, Pauline Kael, holds that "movies, by
    affecting us on sensual and primitive levels, are a supremely
    pleasurable--and dangerous--art form" (xvii).

If the source has two or three authors, give all their names in the text or in the reference:

    Spradley and McCurdy treat both non-Western and Western cultures
    as appropriate concerns of cultural anthropology (1-2).

If the source has more than three authors, give only the first author's name followed by "et al." (the abbreviation for the Latin "and others"):

> Over 100,000 rebels beseiged Peking for nearly two months of 1900 before American, European, and Japanese troops broke through and gained control of the city (Lopez et al. 362).

Sometimes the author's name and page number will not provide enough information for the reader. Such cases include references to one of two or more listed works by the same author and references to one volume of a multivolume work. The following models illustrate how to cite a variety of sources.

#### A GENERAL REFERENCE TO AN ENTIRE WORK

When you cite an entire work rather than a part of it, the reference will not include any page number. If the author's name appears in the text, no parenthetical reference is needed at all. Remember, though, that the source must be included in the list of works cited.

> Boyd deals with the need to acknowledge and come to terms with our fear of nuclear technology.

#### A REFERENCE TO AN ARTICLE OR A ONE-VOLUME BOOK

An article:

> For women prisoners who wanted "to go home (and stay there, if they had husbands) and to go out partying (if they needed a man)," feminism represented "separatism and . . . misandry, male hating" (Gubar and Hedin 780).

A one-volume book:

> Wimsatt and Brooks note the power of Tolstoy's "walloping charicatures of metropolitan fashionable culture" (464).

#### A REFERENCE TO A MULTIVOLUME WORK

If you used only one volume of a multivolume work, your list of works cited can indicate as much by giving the appropriate volume in the entry (see the second entry for Lincoln on p. S-4). However, if you used and listed all the volumes in a multivolume work, your parenthetical reference must specify which volume you are referring to:

> After issuing the Emancipation Proclamation, Lincoln said, "What I did, I did after very full deliberation, and under a very heavy and solemn sense of responsibility" (5: 438).

The number 5 indicates the volume from which the quotation was taken; the number 438 indicates the page number in that volume.

#### A REFERENCE TO ONE WORK BY AN AUTHOR OF TWO OR MORE WORKS

If your list of works cited includes two or more works by the same author, then your reference must tell the reader which of the author's works you are citing. Use the appropriate title or a shortened version of it in the parenthetical reference:

> At about age seven, most children begin to tell stories accurately, describe scenes realistically, and use appropriate gestures to reinforce their story (Gardner, *Arts* 144-45).

The title *Arts* is shortened from Gardner's full title, *The Arts and Human Development* (see the entry for this book on p. S-3). Often, as here, the first main word in the title will be enough to direct the reader to the appropriate source.

#### A REFERENCE TO AN UNSIGNED WORK

Anonymous works are alphabetized by title in the list of works cited. In the text they are referred to by full or shortened title:

> One article predicts that the personal-computer market will not stabilize until at least 1990 ("Notes").

This reference is to an article titled "Notes on Personal Computers." A page reference is unnecessary because the article is no longer than a page (see the entry for the article on p. S-5).

#### A REFERENCE TO A GOVERNMENT DOCUMENT OR A WORK WITH A CORPORATE AUTHOR

If the author of the work is listed as a government body or a corporation, cite the work by the appropriate name. If the name is long, try to work it into the text to avoid an intrusive reference.

> A 1981 report by the United States Department of Labor noted a marked decrease since 1970 in the number of unskilled jobs (19).

#### A REFERENCE TO A LITERARY WORK

Novels, plays, and poems are often available in many editions, so it is helpful to provide information that will allow readers to find the passage you cite no matter what edition they consult. For novels, the page number comes first, followed by information on the appropriate part or chapter of the work:

> Toward the end of James's novel, Maggie suddenly feels "the thick breath of the definite--which was the intimate, the immediate, the familiar, as she hadn't had them for so long" (535; pt. 6, ch. 41).

You can omit page numbers for verse plays and poems, instead citing the appropriate part or act and scene, plus the line number:

> Later in King Lear Shakespeare has the disguised Edgar say, "The prince of darkness is a gentleman" (III.iv.147).

**A REFERENCE TO MORE THAN ONE WORK**

> Two recent articles urge small businesses not to rush to buy a personal computer, even an inexpensive one, on the grounds that a computer badly used is less efficient than no computer at all (Richards 162; Gough and Hall 201).

Since long references in the text can distract the reader, you may choose to cite several or more works in an endnote or footnote rather than in the text. See page S-11.

### Where to place parenthetical references

Generally, place a parenthetical reference at the end of the sentence in which you summarize, paraphrase, or quote a work. The reference should follow a closing quotation mark but precede the sentence punctuation. (See the examples in the previous section.) When a reference pertains to only part of a sentence, place the reference after the material being cited and at the least intrusive point — usually at the end of a clause:

> Though Spelling argues that American automobile manufacturers "have done the best that could be expected" in meeting consumer needs (26), not everyone agrees with him.

When a reference appears at the end of a displayed quotation, place it *outside* the punctuation ending the quotation:

> In Arthur Miller's Death of a Salesman, the most poignant defense of Willie Loman comes from his wife, Linda:
>
>> His name was never in the paper. He's not the finest character that ever lived. But he's a human being, and a terrible thing is happening to him. So attention must be paid. He's not to be allowed to fall into his grave like an old dog. Attention, attention must finally be paid to such a person. (56)

See the sample research paper starting on page S-12 for further examples of placing parenthetical references.

# S3
## Using footnotes or endnotes in special circumstances

Occasionally, you may want to use footnotes or endnotes in place of parenthetical references. If you need to cite several sources at once, listing them in a long parenthetical reference could be intrusive. In that case, signal the citation with a numeral raised above the appropriate line of text and write a note with the same numeral to cite the sources:

**TEXT**     At least five subsequent studies have confirmed these results.[1]

**NOTE**     [1] Abbott and Winger 266-68; Casner 27; Hoyenga 78-79; Marino 36; Tripp, Tripp, and Walk 179-83.

You may also use a footnote or endnote to comment on a source or provide information that does not fit easily in the text:

**TEXT**     So far, no one has succeeded in confirming these results.[2]

**NOTE**     [2] Manter reports spending nearly a year trying to replicate the experiment, but he was never able to produce the high temperatures reported by the original experimenters (616).

In a note the raised numeral is indented five spaces and followed by a space. If it appears as a footnote at the bottom of the appropriate page, set if off from the text with quadruple spacing and single-space the note itself. If it appears as an endnote between the text and the list of works cited, double-space the note and any others grouped with it. (See p. S-32 for an example of an endnote.)

# S4
## Examining a sample research paper

The research paper beginning after this page was prepared by Paul Fuller, the student whose work is followed in Chapter 35. If your instructor asks you to use the documentation system of the *MLA Handbook*, 2nd ed., follow this version of the sample paper instead of the one on pages 492–517.

Facing each page of the paper are comments, keyed by number, on Fuller's use of the system of documentation described above, on the format of the paper, and on the decisions made by Fuller as he moved from research to writing.

How Advertisers Make Us Buy

By

Paul Fuller

English 101, Section A

Mr. R. Macek

March 12, 1982

1. **Title page format.** On his title page Fuller includes the title of his paper about a third of the way down the page, his own name (preceded by *By*) about an inch below the title, and, starting about an inch below his name, some identifying information requested by his instructor (course number, section label, and instructor's name) and the date. He centers all lines in the width of the page and separates them from each other with at least one line of space.

## *Next two pages*

2. **Outline format.** If your instructor asks you to include your final outline, place it between the title page and the text, as Fuller does on the following pages. You may leave its pages unnumbered, or you may number them with small Roman numerals, as Fuller does. If you number the outline pages, omit the number on the first page and begin numbering with *ii* on the second page. Place the heading "Outline" at the top of the first page.
3. **Outline content.** Fuller includes his final thesis sentence as part of his outline so that his instructor can see how the parts relate to the whole.
4. Fuller casts his final outline in full sentences. Some instructors request topic outlines, in which ideas appear in phrases instead of in sentences and do not end with periods.
5. Notice that each main division (numbered with Roman numerals) refers directly to a portion of the thesis sentence and that all the subdivisions relate directly to their main division. Notice, too, the use of parallel phrasing for parallel levels. You need not repeat words such as *advertisers say,* but in this case they help Fuller relate his ideas to each other logically and clearly.

Outline

Thesis: Advertisers appeal to consumers' emotions, rather than to their reason, because consumers choose products irrationally.

I. Critics of advertising say advertisers deliberately use strong emotional and irrational appeals.
   A. Marshall McLuhan says the appeals of advertising are directed to the unconscious.
   B. Vance Packard says the methods of advertisers represent regression for the rational nature of human beings.
   C. David Ogilvy says that most advertising treats consumers as if they were idiots, unable to reason.

II. Advertisers say they appeal to emotion because consumers choose products irrationally.
   A. Advertisers say that advertising by its nature as human communication expresses both emotional and rational messages.
   B. Advertisers say human beings choose irrationally.
   C. Advertisers say that appealing to emotion increases sales.
      1. Adding color to products or their ads increases sales.

ii

        2. Adding cartoon characters to products or their packages increases sales.

        3. Adding emotional symbols to ads increases sales.

III. Studies of advertising indicate that advertisers do appeal to emotions, as both critics and advertisers claim, and that consumers seem to choose products emotionally, as advertisers claim.

    A. An informal survey of ads indicates that the average ad uses much more emotional appeal than rational appeal.

    B. Experiments by independent researchers suggest that consumers respond to emotional appeals in advertising and that they do not examine ads rationally.

        1. One study showed that consumers make an emotional choice in favor of ads that merely sound truthful.

        2. Another study showed that consumers do not examine ads rationally, but do respond emotionally to a claim that merely sounds rational.

How Advertisers Make Us Buy

    Against a background of rolling music and a deep voice speaking of "winning the world," a woman descends from a swirl of sailcloth and clouds. This view widens to take in the whole scene--ship, ocean, sky--in a panorama that seems cosmic. The purpose of this drama is to make a television audience buy some coffee. The advertisement's outsized play for emotional attention and response is typical of contemporary advertising. Critics of such advertising accuse it of ignoring the human capacity for reason, the ability to make purchasing decisions on the basis of a product's performance and quality, while appealing instead to consumers' emotions about humor, sex, status, and adventure and to their unquestioning faith in science. In fact, advertisers do appeal to consumers' emotions, rather than to their reason, because consumers choose products irrationally.

    The critics of advertising stress its manipulativeness and mindlessness. Marshall McLuhan, the philosopher of mass-media culture, says that advertising directs its appeals to the unconscious:

        Ours is the first age in which many thousands of
        the best-trained individual minds have made it a
        full-time business to get inside the collective
        public mind . . . to manipulate, exploit, con-

6. **Title.** Although a title such as "Appeals to Emotion in Advertising" would reflect Fuller's thesis more accurately, it would also be less forceful. **Paper format.** The title is typed two inches from the top of the page and is separated from the text by four lines of space.
7. **Introduction.** Fuller opens by summarizing a television commercial to demonstrate how illogical advertising can be and to introduce readers to the issues of the thesis. The example is concrete and effective. However, Fuller could have begun his paper without it by rephrasing the first sentence after the word *coffee:* "Outsized plays for emotional attention and response are typical of contemporary advertising." The following sentence elaborates on this idea while also introducing advertising's critics and clarifying two central terms of the thesis sentence and the entire paper: *appeal to reason* and *appeal to emotion.*
8. **Relation to outline.** This paragraph corresponds to Part I of Fuller's outline. Part II of the outline begins with the next paragraph and continues until page 4 of the paper.
9. **Introducing quotations.** Fuller effectively introduces his quotations here and on the next two pages: He establishes the credentials of each author in an identifying phrase; he summarizes each author's point of view; and, with the shorter quotation from Packard, he integrates the author's sentence structure into his own. (But see also comment 14, p. S-19, on the Ogilvy quotation.)
10. **Format of long quotations.** The McLuhan and Ogilvy quotations on this page and the next exceed four typed lines, so Fuller sets these off from the text. These block quotations are set off by triple spacing above and below, are themselves double-spaced, and are indented ten spaces from the left margin.
11. **Editing quotations.** Fuller uses ellipses in the two long quotations to show that he has eliminated irrelevant material (see 25e). All the ellipses consist of three spaced periods; but the second one in the McLuhan quotation is preceded by a sentence period closed up to the last word, and the ellipsis in the Ogilvy quotation is followed by a space and a comma from the original. Fuller's editing of the McLuhan quotation is not entirely successful. The sentence after the ellipsis strays from the idea Fuller wants to capture (that advertising appeals are directed to the unconscious), so he should have omitted it as well.

2

trol. . . . Why not assist the public to observe consciously the drama intended to operate unconsciously? (v)

Vance Packard, who brought national attention to the manipulations of advertisers in his best-selling <u>The Hidden Persuaders</u>, asserts that the methods of advertisers "represent regress rather than progress for man in his long struggle to become a rational and self-guiding being" (4). David Ogilvy, one of advertising's most famous successes, concedes that most advertising treats consumers as if they were unable to reason:

> When I first began making advertisements . . . , I looked at the so-called mass magazines and I was impressed by the extraordinary gap between editorial content and advertising content. I saw that the editors were writing with taste to an intelligent audience, and the advertising writers were writing to idiots. (qtd. in Glatzer 85)

Advertisers themselves say that ads combine rational and emotional appeals (Bernstein 295). This mixture, they claim, comes from advertising's nature as another form of human communication. Regular conversation illustrates how all human communication, including advertising, works. In regular conversation <u>how</u> something is said is often as important as <u>what</u> is said. The speaker's voice, gestures, and facial expression carry emotional messages just as important as the rational content of what the speaker says.

12. **Reference when the author is named in the text.** Fuller has already mentioned McLuhan's name in the text, so he does not repeat it in the reference. Since this is a displayed quotation, the reference falls outside the closing punctuation. In contrast, the reference for Packard in the next sentence falls between the closing quotation mark and the sentence period.
13. **Paragraphing.** Fuller does not begin a new paragraph after the McLuhan quotation because the following material (the Packard and Ogilvy quotations) is directly related. After the Ogilvy quotation, Fuller does begin a new paragraph because he's embarking on a new thought.
14. **Reference to an indirect source.** Fuller's reference indicates that he discovered the Ogilvy quotation in Glatzer's book. **Indirect sources.** Glatzer quotes from Ogilvy's autobiography, a widely available source that Fuller should have consulted directly. A writer should avoid quoting a source secondhand unless the firsthand source cannot be located. In this case, the work of "one of advertising's most famous successes," as Fuller identifies Ogilvy, might have provided significant information. See also comments 30 and 32 on pages S-29 and S-31.
15. **Reference when the author is not named in the text.** Because Fuller has not used Bernstein's name in the text, he provides it in the reference. **Citing and introducing paraphrases.** Fuller is summarizing Bernstein, so he cites the source as he would the source of a quotation. The rest of this paragraph is a paraphrase from another source cited at the end (next page). Fuller has put the parenthetical reference in the right place, but he has failed to introduce the lengthy paraphrase adequately. As a result, the second sentence ("This mixture, they claim, . . .") appears to be undocumented, and the reference seems to document only the last sentence in the paragraph. Fuller should have introduced the paraphrase in the second sentence and then made it clear that other sentences in the paragraph derive from the same source: *"Advertiser Pierre Martineau claims* that the mixture comes from advertising's nature as another form of human communication. *He notes* that regular conversation. . . ." With Martineau's name in the text, the parenthetical reference would require only page numbers.

*Supplement*

In printed advertising, art, layout, and typeface carry the emotional messages. In television advertising, the personalities of announcers and actors, the music, and the visual imagery become symbols of emotional meaning (Martineau 139-40).

Advertisers maintain that their emotional appeals are appropriate because human beings are essentially irrational. Car salespeople have noticed that customers on the verge of buying an expensive car for an emotional motive, such as a desire for status, like to talk at the last minute about superior performance in order to justify their emotional decision with a rational motive (Smith 6). Pierre Martineau explains this behavior more generally:

> The entire personality of every individual is built around basic emotional needs, and the whole system of his thinking is determined by these needs, even though superficially the individual defends his point of view on purely rational grounds. Experiments repeatedly show that his rationality is highly selective rationality (or in other words, not rational at all). (62; emphasis added)

Other recent studies confirm the same view of consumers by advertisers.[1]

Advertisers claim many sales successes through appeals to emotion. One technique for increasing the emotional appeal of products is "color engineering." Adding color to

16. **Summary statement.** This sentence does not contain a reference because it is Fuller's summary of evidence from the sources cited in the rest of the paragraph.
17. **Paraphrasing.** Fuller paraphrases the example about car salespeople even though his note card contains the exact quotation from the source. He decides not to quote directly because he can reduce several sentences in the original to one of his own, and he does not want two long quotations in a row. Here is the original note card:

> Consumers' irrational choices
> Smith, *Motivation Research*, p. 6.
> "Car salesmen joke that their product knowledge — performance statistics, repair record, etc. — doesn't make them a dime. What sells an expensive car is the customer's feeling about luxury, good looks, status. So he does not appear impulsive, the customer may ask about performance just as he is about to sign the papers, but at that moment the salesman could say almost anything without jeopardizing what is essentially an irrational purchase."

18. **Adding emphasis to quotations.** Fuller underlines certain words in the quotation that reinforce his thesis especially clearly. He acknowledges this change inside the parenthetical reference, separated by a semicolon from the page number.
19. **Using an endnote for supplementary information.** Instead of continuing to quote and paraphrase the same view of consumers, Fuller lets readers know that further support is available, and the raised numeral ([1]) signals that he has more to say at a note with the corresponding numeral. See page S-32 for the note itself.
20. **Selecting supporting evidence.** In these paragraphs listing sales successes that resulted from appeals to emotion, Fuller has selected from his sources the most dramatic and vivid success stories he found. He provides concrete facts that support his case. And he carefully cites his sources.

4

an ad or to a product in which color has no practical function increases sales. For example, until the 1920s fountain pens were made of hard black rubber. When colored plastic pens were introduced, sales improved "astronomically" (Ketcham 7). Using aluminum paint instead of black on bedsprings improved sales by 25 percent for one manufacturer (Ketcham 8). A Gloucester fish packer increased his sales 33 percent simply by adding color to his advertising circular (Hotchkiss 164). Currently, the emotional appeal of cartoon characters increases sales 10 to 20 percent when the characters are printed on products or their packages (Johnson). Experts disagree on just why color and cartoons have such appeal; for instance, the cartoons may trigger hero worship or nostalgia (Johnson). Clearly, however, the appeal is emotional and sales improve because of it.

    Two classic advertising campaigns that relied on emotional appeals are Hathaway's and Marlboro's. After ads for Hathaway shirts began to include a well-built, mysterious man with a patch over one eye, sales of the shirts tripled (Martineau 148). The manufacturers of Marlboro cigarettes experienced an even more dramatic increase in sales because of a change in advertising. In 1954 Philip Morris decided to enter one of its worst-selling cigarettes, Marlboro, in the new filter-tip market (Glatzer 122-23). To change the product's image as a woman's cigarette, the advertisers eliminated all women from the ads and substituted virile men. Each new ad emphasized a tattoo on the hand of the man smoking a Marlboro. The tattoos were a symbol that seemed

21. **Going back to sources.** In his first draft Fuller described his examples of sales successes with phrases like "sales increased" and "sales improved" rather than with actual figures, and his assertions lacked force. When he realized he needed to be more specific, he referred to his bibliography cards (showing the call numbers) and to his note cards (showing page numbers) and was able to collect the figures he wanted in a quick trip to the library. In the note card below Fuller has added to the information originally gathered from the article by Johnson.

---

Johnson, "The Cartoon Creature," p. 3. <u>Increasing sales by stressing emotion</u>

Printing cartoon characters — Mickey Mouse, Snoopy, Superman — on products or packages can significantly <u>increase</u> sales.

(average increase 10–20%, can be 50–100%)

---

22. **Reference to a one-page article.** Johnson's article appears on only one page of the newspaper it is in, and Fuller gives that page number in the list of works cited (see p. S-34). Thus he does not need to repeat the page number in the reference.
23. **Using sources effectively.** In this paragraph Fuller blends material from two sources to make one point about the success of emotional appeals. Instead of merely stringing together other people's ideas, he arranges the material in order of increasing drama and thus shapes his research to express and support his own views. Notice that Fuller's four references (two for each source) indicate clearly which information came from which source.

to give the whole ad campaign an emotional unity (Martineau 147). This shift in emotional appeal improved Marlboro's sales drastically: from near zero in 1954 to 6.4 billion in 1955, 14.3 billion in 1956, and 19.5 billion in 1957 (Glatzer 134).

But advertisers' success stories are not the last word. An informal survey and more formal studies of advertising show that appeals to emotion predominate and that consumers seem to go out of their way to make choices for emotional reasons.

My own informal survey of ads in an issue of Newsweek revealed that most of the ads (thirty of forty-two) used a predominantly emotional appeal (see Table 1, next page). Only one-fifth of the ads (nine of forty-two) depended on rational appeal as much as 50 percent. Some ads of products for which rational appeal would be easy or likely--products such as a newsletter, an economy car, and insurance--barely used appeals to reason (under 20 percent rational appeal). This limited (one-reader, one-magazine) study leads to several conclusions: (1) that most ads appeal primarily to consumers' emotions; (2) that only a tiny fraction of ads (one of forty-two) appeal primarily to reason; and (3) that no ads use rational appeal 100 percent, although many (twelve of forty-two) use emotional appeal 100 percent.

In an experimental study of advertising, Robert Settle and Linda Golden found that admitting a product's inferiority on one or two minor points of comparison was more effective in advertising than claiming the product's superiority on

24. **Transitional paragraph and relation to outline.** Here Fuller devotes a paragraph to the transition between Part II and Part III of the outline, between sales evidence supporting advertisers' claims about consumers and equally supportive studies by nonadvertisers.
25. **Original research.** Because he is a consumer, Fuller feels that his subjective reactions to ads are legitimate responses to evaluate and use. Nevertheless, he wisely admits the limitations of his survey. **Primary and secondary sources.** Fuller's study of magazine ads is a primary source because it is direct, firsthand information. His other sources are secondary because they contain other people's reports and interpretations of primary or secondary sources. In several instances he relies on secondhand sources when he should have used original sources; see comments 14 (p. S-19), 30 (p. S-29), and 32 (p. S-31).
26. **Reference to illustration.** Here Fuller refers specifically to the table that shows the complete results of his survey.
27. **Reporting studies.** Fuller's descriptions of experiments here are detailed enough to let readers know how the experiments were conducted, yet not so detailed that readers will get bogged down in the experiments and lose track of his ideas. Again, as in presenting the examples of successful advertising campaigns earlier, Fuller arranges material in order of increasing detail and drama. He might have enlivened his description by including more quotations from the studies as well as even more specific information (such as some of the products evaluated in the first study). He had the specific details on his note card but failed to use them.

---

Gregg, "To Sell Your Product," p. 35.

Repts. study by Robert Settle and Linda Golden in *Jnl. of Marketing Research* 11 (May 1974). 120 bus. students evaluated fictitious ads for a pen, a watch, a blender, a camera, and a clock radio. Half the ads claimed the product was five ways superior to a well-known competitor; the other half claimed superiority on only three points and inferiority on two points. 80% of students found ads admitting some inferiority to be more persuasive.

---

See also comment 30, page S-29.

TABLE 1

SURVEY OF ADVERTISEMENTS IN NEWSWEEK, 19 FEBRUARY 1979[a]

| Advertisement | Percentages Emotional/Rational | Advertisement | Percentages Emotional/Rational |
|---|---|---|---|
| Tobacco Institute | 100/0 | Jameson Irish Whiskey | 100/0 |
| American Forest Institute | 50/50 | Jack Daniels | 90/10 |
| Jeep | 80/20 | Ronrico Rum | 90/10 |
| Datsun | 60/40 | Canadian Club | 100/0 |
| Horizon TC3 | 90/10 | Royal copier | 60/40 |
| MGB | 80/20 | Sharp copier | 50/50 |
| Ford Pinto | 60/40 | Mutual Life Insurance | 100/0 |
| VW | 100/0 | Sun Life Insurance | 100/0 |
| Winnebago | 80/20 | GE TV | 10/90 |
| Exxon | 50/50 | Vivitar lens | 50/50 |
| Lonestar Building Supplier | 80/20 | Book ad | 95/5 |
| Alcoa aluminum | 50/50 | Famolare shoes | 50/50 |
| Tareyton | 100/0 | Trinity missions | 100/0 |
| L&M Lights | 50/50 | St. Elizabeth Hotel | 90/10 |
| Marlboro | 100/0 | Newsletter on new products | 80/20 |
| Doral II | 90/10 | Anderson Windowwalls | 50/50 |
| Merit | 80/20 | Anacin | 50/50 |
| Winston Lights | 100/0 | Preparation H | 50/50 |
| Salem | 100/0 | United Cerebral Palsy | 100/0 |
| Beechcraft Aviation | 80/20 | | |
| Pan Am | 50/50 | | |
| Pakistan Airlines | 80/20 | | |
| Chivas Regal | 90/10 | | |

[a]My method for determining what percentage of an ad appealed to emotion and what percentage to reason involved (1) recording the overall impact of the ad as emotional or rational; (2) evaluating the proportions of space given to different purposes and the effects of layout, color, type, and artwork; (3) thinking of the possible ways to advertise the product without appealing to emotions and evaluating the ad against these; and (4) weighing my observations and assigning percentages to emotional and rational appeals. As an example, the Ronrico Rum ad contains an illustration occupying 80 percent of the space. It shows an upright bottle of rum (label facing out) and the shape of a bottle, tilted at 60°, containing a photograph of a couple kissing, palm trees, beautiful water--a scene whose greenness stands out against the mostly white ad and the pale bottle of rum. The angle of the bottle outline suggests it is about to fall and makes the viewer want to reach out and grab it. The ad's brief copy discusses the rum's "authentic" relation with Puerto Rico. Only the words "smooth, light taste" describe a rationally desirable quality of rum. I rated the ad (perhaps generously) 90 percent emotional, 10 percent rational.

28. **Table format.** Fuller places the table after the table reference (p. 5 of the paper) and on a separate sheet of paper. He numbers the table with an Arabic numeral (1) and capitalizes both the label and the title. The title tells readers what magazine the advertisements appeared in. His column headings clearly label the information beneath them. Generally, tables like this one should be double-spaced throughout, but Fuller single-spaces his so it fits on one page.
29. **Source acknowledgment.** Since the table contains Fuller's original material, no acknowledgment (source note) is needed. If one were, the source would be given immediately after the table and preceded by the word "source" and a colon. **Explanatory note.** Fuller's table does need an explanation of his method so that readers can judge the value of his survey. The note is keyed as a footnote, but a raised letter ([a]) is used instead of a raised number to prevent possible confusion of text notes with the table note.

all counts. The researchers asked 120 business students to evaluate a series of ads. (The products advertised were fictitious.) Half the ads claimed that the fictitious product was superior to the best-selling and well-known actual product on five points of comparison. The other half claimed the fictitious product was superior on only three counts and inferior on two minor points. The students found the latter ads, which admitted some inferiority, to be more successful in persuading them to buy the new (fictitious) product instead of the best seller (Gregg). They made an emotional choice in favor of ads that simply sounded truthful without having evidence that the claims of truth were in fact valid.

In another study with experimental ads, Seymour Lieberman had an advertising agency create two television ads for each of six fictitious products. Each product had one deceitful ad containing a false or made-up scientific claim and one truthful ad that did not contain the scientific claim. For instance, the deceitful ad for a fictitious plant fertilizer stressed that the fertilizer contained protein (though in fact protein does not help plants grow), whereas the truthful ad did not mention protein. The deceitful ad for a fictitious bunion remedy stated that the remedy contained "four times as much methylglyoxal" (although methylglyoxal does not help treat bunions), whereas the truthful ad did not mention methylglyoxal. Both pairs of ads used the same actors and the same language; the only difference was the presence or absence of the scientific claim. After being asked to say which products interested them, one hundred middle-income

30. **Original and secondhand sources.** Fuller's reference here indicates that his information on Settle and Gordon's study comes from Gregg's article. (See the note card below.) Instead of relying on a secondhand report of the study, Fuller should have consulted the original article by Settle and Gordon, not only to ensure the accuracy of his description but also to check for additional information. (Note that Fuller omits page numbers from the Gregg reference because the information appeared on both pages of a two-page article.) **Drawing conclusions.** Fuller places references to Gregg and to the article "Truth Doesn't Sell" (next page of the paper) after his descriptions of the experiments but before the conclusions he draws to support the second part of his thesis (that consumers choose products irrationally). In fact, the experimenters did not use their results for quite the same purposes as Fuller does. For example, a note card on Gregg's article quotes the researchers' conclusion:

> Gregg, "To Sell Your Product," *Psych. Today*, p. 36. Research on consumer responses—conclusions
>
> Quoting Robert Settle and Linda Golden from their article in *Jnl. of Marketing Research* 11 (May 1974). "Advertisers [should] disclaim at least one feature of minor importance" rather than "exclude it from the message entirely." They can thus "make advertising claims of superiority more believable."

By separating the studies' results from his own conclusions about the results, Fuller demonstrates the amount of thought he has given his sources, and he hopes to avoid misrepresenting them (always a danger in reporting and interpreting the work of others). However, since Fuller's conclusions are not those of the researchers, he might have mentioned briefly the researchers' goals and conclusions so that his readers could evaluate his use of their results.

31. **Use of quotation.** Fuller's quotation of a key phrase from the study makes his description more concrete and also illustrates how successfully the researchers imitated real ads in their fictitious ones. As noted in comment 27 (p. S-25), Fuller might have made greater use of such quotations and details from the studies he cites.

consumers watched the deceitful ads and another hundred middle-income consumers watched the truthful ads. More consumers showed interest in the deceitful fertilizer ad than showed interest in the truthful ad. And four times as many consumers showed interest in the deceitful four-times-as-much methylglyoxal ad for a bunion remedy as showed interest in the truthful ad. Similar results occurred with two of the other four pairs of ads tested ("Truth"). The consumers did not examine the ads' claims rationally. Instead, they gravitated to what sounded like fact, responding emotionally to claims of scientific improvements without rationally evaluating the claims.

The critics of advertising accuse advertisers of using emotional appeals deliberately and irresponsibly. They imply that consumers would make rational decisions about products if the ads for those products gave them facts about performance and quality on which to base a rational choice. Advertisers freely admit their emphasis on emotional appeals but maintain that consumers make choices irrationally. As proof, they offer the sales successes brought about by purely emotional appeals. One informal survey verifies advertisers' reliance on emotional appeals. And formal experiments suggest that consumers do not require hard information on which to base decisions but will accept the appearance of truth or fact as a substitute for the real thing. We may say we object to the overblown advertisement with no informative content. That is certainly the kind of ad we see most often. But it also seems to be the kind of ad we deserve.

32. **Reference to an unsigned article.** Here Fuller acknowledges an unsigned article titled "Truth Doesn't Sell" (see the entry for this source on p. S-34). Shortening the title to "Truth" provides adequate information for readers to locate the source while keeping the reference as unobtrusive as possible. Fuller draws on information appearing on both pages of the two-page article, so a page number is not needed in the reference. **Original and secondhand sources.** Again, as with the article by Gregg (comment 30, p. S-29), Fuller relies on a secondhand report of the study he describes. He should have consulted the original report by Lieberman.
33. **Conclusion.** Fuller's conclusion might be faulted for lack of imagination, but it suits his purpose. He shows that his thesis is valid by summarizing the evidence he has presented in the paper. In his last few sentences he switches to *we* in a way that emphasizes the relevance of his conclusion for himself and his readers. His last sentence provides a final edge.

## Note

[1] See, for example, Engle, Kollats, and Blackwell 58. There the same idea is stated in a complex diagram, the "Complete Model of Consumer Behavior Showing Purchasing Processes and Outcomes." Out of twenty-three boxes of factors only one box, "Evaluative Criteria," seems to represent rationality.

34. **Format of notes.** The word "Note" is centered two inches from the top of the page and is followed by four lines of space. (The heading would be plural — "Notes" — if Fuller had more than one note.) The note itself is double-spaced. The first line is indented five spaces and preceded by a raised number corresponding to the number used in the text. A space separates the number and the note.
35. **Endnote for additional relevant information.** Fuller's single note provides an example of work confirming that advertisers view consumers as irrational. (See p. S-20 for the note reference in Fuller's text.) Fuller cites the last names of all three authors, and he provides a page number (58) directing readers to the appropriate place in the source.

                                                          10
                            Works Cited

Bernstein, David. *Creative Advertising*. London: Longman,
     1974.

Engel, James F., David T. Kollats, and Roger D. Blackwell.
     *Consumer Behavior*. 2nd ed. New York: Holt, 1973.

Glatzer, Robert. *The New Advertising: The Great Campaigns*.
     New York: Citadel, 1970.

Gregg, Gary. "To Sell Your Product, Admit It's Not Perfect."
     *Psychology Today* Oct. 1974: 35-36.

Hotchkiss, George Burton. *An Outline of Advertising: Its
     Philosophy, Science, Art, and Strategy*. 3rd ed. New
     York: Macmillan, 1950.

Johnson, Sharon. "The Cartoon Creature as Salesman." *The
     New York Times* 11 Feb. 1979, sec. 3: 3.

Ketcham, Howard. *Color Planning: For Business and Industry*.
     New York: Harper, 1958.

McLuhan, Herbert Marshall. *The Mechanical Bride: Folklore
     of Industrial Man*. Boston: Beacon, 1951.

Martineau, Pierre. *Motivation in Advertising: Motives That
     Make People Buy*. New York: McGraw-Hill, 1957.

Packard, Vance. *The Hidden Persuaders*. New York: Pocket
     Books, 1958.

Smith, George H. *Motivation Research in Advertising and
     Marketing*. 1954. Westport: Greenwood, 1971.

"Truth Doesn't Sell." *Time* 14 May 1973: 96-97.

36. **Format of list of works cited.** The heading "Works Cited" is centered two inches from the top of the page and followed by four lines of space. The entries are double-spaced. The first line of each entry begins at the left margin; subsequent lines of the same entry are indented five spaces. The entries are alphabetized.
37. Typical entry for a **book with one author.**
38. Entry for a **book with three authors** in an **edition other than the first.** Here is Fuller's bibliography card for this source:

---

HF 541
.7
.E5

    Engel, James F., David T. Kollats, and
    Roger D. Blackwell. <u>Consumer
    Behavior</u>. 2nd ed. New York:
    Holt, 1973.

---

39. Entry for a **signed article in a monthly periodical.**
40. Entry for a **signed article in a daily newspaper.**
41. Entry for a **republished book.**
42. Entry for an **unsigned article in a weekly magazine.** Here is Fuller's bibliography card for this source:

---

    "Truth Doesn't Sell." <u>Time</u>
    14 May 1973: 96-97.

---